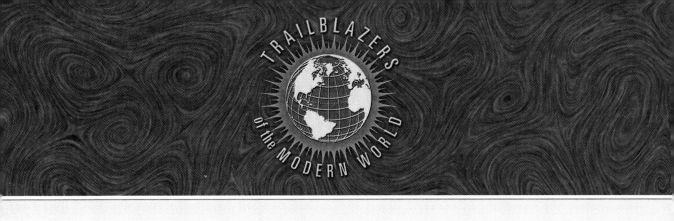

FRANKLIN D. ROOSEVELT

By Robin Doak

WORLD ALMANAC® LIBRARY

Please visit our web site at: www.worldalmanaclibrary.com
For a free color catalog describing World Almanac® Library's
list of high-quality books and multimedia programs,
call 1-800-848-2928 or fax your request to (414) 332-3567.

Library of Congress Cataloging-in-Publication Data

Doak, Robin.
    Franklin Delano Roosevelt / by Robin Doak.
        p. cm. — (Trailblazers of the modern world)
    Includes bibliographical references and index.
    Summary: A biography of the thirty-second president, who led the United States during the Depression and World War II.
    ISBN 0-8368-5073-4 (lib. bdg.)
    ISBN 0-8368-5233-8 (softcover)
    1. Roosevelt, Franklin D. (Franklin Delano), 1882-1945—Juvenile literature.   2. Presidents—United States—Biography—
Juvenile literature.   [1. Roosevelt, Franklin D. (Franklin Delano), 1882-1945.   2. Presidents.] I. Title. II. Series.
    E807.D58   2002
    973.917'092—dc21
    [B]   2001045626

This North American edition first published in 2002 by
World Almanac® Library
330 West Olive Street, Suite 100
Milwaukee, WI 53212 USA

An Editorial Directions book
Editor: Lucia Raatma
Designer and page production: Ox and Company
Photo researcher: Dawn Friedman
Indexer: Tim Griffin
World Almanac® Library art direction: Tammy Gruenewald
World Almanac® Library production: Susan Ashley and Jessica L. Yanke

Photo credits: Hulton Archive, cover; Franklin D. Roosevelt Library Digital Archives, 4; AP/Wide World Photos, 5;
Hulton Archive/New York Times Company, 6 top; Hulton Archive, 6 bottom; Corbis, 7 top; Hulton Archive/Pach
Brothers, 7 bottom; Corbis, 8; Franklin D. Roosevelt Library Digital Archives, 9 top; Corbis/Bettmann, 9 bottom, 10;
Corbis, 11, 12 top; Corbis/Bettmann, 12 bottom; AP/Wide World Photos, 14 top; Corbis/Bettmann, 14 bottom, 15; Hulton
Archive, 16 top; Franklin D. Roosevelt Library Digital Archives, 16 bottom; AP/Wide World Photos, 17; Hulton Archive,
19, 20; AP/Wide World Photos, 21; Franklin D. Roosevelt Library Digital Archives, 22 top; Corbis/Bettmann, 22 bottom;
AP/Wide World Photos, 23; Hulton Archive/Lewis W. Hine/George Eastman House, 24; Hulton Archive, 25; AP/Wide
World Photos, 26; Corbis/Bettmann, 28; Hulton Archive, 30, 32; Corbis, 33; AP/Wide World Photos, 34; Hulton Archive,
35; Hulton Archive/U.S. Library of Congress, 36; Hulton Archive/American Stock, 37; AP/Wide World Photos, 38;
Hulton Archive, 39 top; Corbis, 39 bottom; Hulton Archive, 40 top; AP/Wide World Photos, 40 bottom, 41; Hulton
Archive, 43 top; Hulton Archive/IMDB/ Richard Ellis, 43 bottom.

Printed in the United States of America

1 2 3 4 5 6 7 8 9 06 05 04 03 02

TABLE of CONTENTS

Words that appear in the glossary are printed in **boldface**
type the first time they occur in the text.

CHAPTER 1

A GREAT PRESIDENT

Franklin Delano Roosevelt had an optimism that guided the United States through difficult times.

Franklin Delano Roosevelt was the thirty-second president of the United States. He overcame a disabling illness to become one of the greatest presidents in the history of the country. Elected to an unprecedented four terms, he guided the country through some of the worst periods in its history. During his twelve years in office, he was looked at as a father figure and friend by many Americans. At the same time, Roosevelt was detested by some who felt he had too much power and was hostile toward big business and the wealthy. These people referred to him as "that man in the White House." Today, Roosevelt is remembered by historians as one of the most effective presidents of all time.

A RAY OF HOPE

In the 1930s, the United States was suffering from the **Great Depression**, the country's worst crisis since the Civil War. In 1932, Americans chose Roosevelt to lead them out of this challenging time. Known to the masses simply as "FDR," Roosevelt had about him an air of optimism and a dynamic personality that brightened even the darkest hours of the Great

Depression. His faith in democracy and the United States gave people hope for the future.

During Roosevelt's first term in office, he worked with Congress to pass legislation that would help Americans in need and reform the economy. His first 100 days in office set a benchmark of activity and progress for every president who followed him. The effects of these laws have been great and long-lasting. Some of the measures, such as Social Security, still survive today.

Roosevelt made the federal government responsible for its citizens in a way it had never been before. He also made the presidency a strong branch of the government, a tradition that continues.

Many homeless people lived in cardboard boxes or shacks during the Great Depression.

COMMANDER IN CHIEF

When World War II began in 1939, Roosevelt faced his second major crisis as president. The president stated that he wanted to keep the United States out of the war. At the same time, however, he wanted to help countries that were being attacked by aggressive nations, so he began a military buildup in the United States. When the United States finally entered the war in 1941, Roosevelt provided strong leadership. He worked with Great Britain and the **Soviet Union** to win the war and dictate the terms of Germany's surrender.

In his final years, Roosevelt also helped lay the groundwork for the United Nations, the global peacekeeping organization that still exists today. When he died in April 1945, people around the world mourned the passing of one of the greatest statesmen who had ever lived.

CHAPTER 2

YOUNG FRANKLIN

Franklin at age seven

Franklin D. Roosevelt with his parents in the early 1900s

Franklin Delano Roosevelt was born in Hyde Park, New York, on January 30, 1882, into a life of luxury and privilege. The only child of James and Sara Delano Roosevelt, he was doted on from the moment he was born, especially by his mother. Franklin grew up surrounded by wealth on the family's Hyde Park estate. His mother took charge of his early education, hiring governesses and teachers to tutor the young boy at home. For fun, Franklin rode ponies, played tennis, collected stamps, and vacationed in Europe.

From an early age, Franklin's parents taught him that the special privileges of the wealthy carried with them a weighty responsibility. His father, a staunch Democrat, believed that the rich had an obligation to help those who were less fortunate by performing good deeds and civic duties. This was a lesson Franklin would never forget.

SCHOOL DAYS

When Franklin was fourteen, his parents sent him to the exclusive Groton School in Massachusetts. Here, Roosevelt proved to be an average student. He was very interested in sports and signed up for football and baseball. Although he was not immediately accepted by his peers at Groton, Roosevelt worked hard to make friends.

When Franklin graduated from Groton in 1900, he enrolled at Harvard University in Cambridge, Massachusetts. At that time, Franklin's cousin, Republican Theodore "Teddy" Roosevelt, was vice president of the United States. In 1901, Teddy became president after the assassination of President William McKinley. Roosevelt admired his older cousin and looked to him as a role model. His Harvard years marked the beginning of Franklin's love for politics. His time at Harvard was also one of sadness, though, because Franklin's father died when he was just a freshman.

After graduating from Harvard in 1903, Franklin completed a year of graduate studies there, and in 1904, he entered Columbia Law School. Three years later, he passed his bar exams and took a job as a clerk in a New York law firm. Despite this law education, Franklin quickly realized that he had absolutely no interest in being a lawyer. His real interest lay in following in the footsteps of his famous cousin, Teddy. Franklin wanted to be a politician.

The Roosevelt estate at Hyde Park is now a museum.

Franklin's famous cousin President Theodore Roosevelt

In 1903, twenty-one-year-old Franklin shocked his mother with the news that he wanted to marry a young woman named Anna Eleanor Roosevelt. Eleanor was a distant cousin of Franklin's, but this was not what upset his mother. Sara felt that Eleanor and her son were too young to be married. First, she asked the two to keep the engagement secret for a year. Then she promptly took her son off on a Caribbean cruise, hoping he would change his mind.

Franklin did not change his mind, though, and on St. Patrick's Day in 1905, he and Eleanor were married. Eleanor's uncle, President Theodore Roosevelt, gave the bride away—and captured most of the attention at the wedding. In 1906, Eleanor gave birth to Anna, the first of the couple's six children.

Franklin the Troublemaker

When fourteen-year-old Franklin arrived at the Groton School, he was starting two years later than the other boys there. Most of his classmates had enrolled at the age of twelve. These boys had already been together for two years and had made friends. Many of the boys at the prestigious prep school felt that Franklin, the new kid on the block, was too well behaved and serious. Franklin, however, was determined to gain their respect and admiration. During his first year at the school, he was thrilled to finally receive his first punishment for misbehaving in class. In a letter to his parents, he wrote: "I have served off my first black-mark today, and am very glad I got it, as I was thought to have no school-spirit before." "Serving off a black mark" meant performing a chore such as mowing the lawn or shoveling snow.

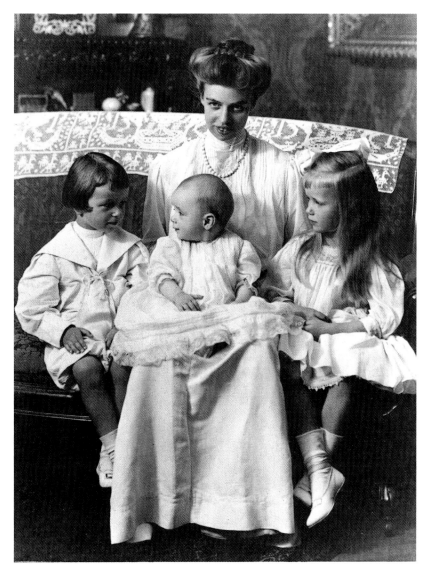

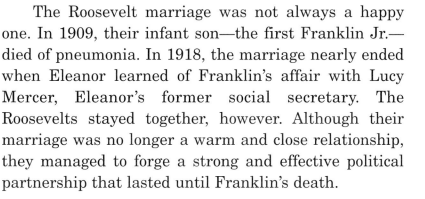

The Roosevelt marriage was not always a happy one. In 1909, their infant son—the first Franklin Jr.—died of pneumonia. In 1918, the marriage nearly ended when Eleanor learned of Franklin's affair with Lucy Mercer, Eleanor's former social secretary. The Roosevelts stayed together, however. Although their marriage was no longer a warm and close relationship, they managed to forge a strong and effective political partnership that lasted until Franklin's death.

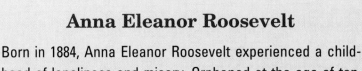

Anna Eleanor Roosevelt

Born in 1884, Anna Eleanor Roosevelt experienced a childhood of loneliness and misery. Orphaned at the age of ten, Eleanor considered herself awkward, plain, and unloved. As a governor's wife, and later as America's First Lady, Eleanor championed the causes of the poor and the persecuted. Over the years, she became one of the most admired women in the world.

During her husband's four terms as U.S. president, Eleanor revolutionized the role of First Lady. She acted as her husband's eyes and ears, keeping him well informed about the social problems of the day. She was also a strong advocate for women, blacks, workers, and many other groups. Beginning in 1936, Eleanor wrote a popular newspaper column called "My Day" to let the public know what she was up to. She continued to write the column until 1962.

Eleanor cared deeply about the world around her. In 1943, she wrote: "At all times, day by day, we have to continue fighting for freedom of religion, freedom of speech, freedom from want—for these are things that must be gained in peace as well as in war."

SUCCESS AND TRAGEDY

Roosevelt got his first crack at politics in 1910 when he was asked to run as a Democrat for a seat in the New York state senate. Only one Democrat had held the seat since 1856, so Roosevelt's chances for victory seemed slim, but he took up the challenge with relish. He rented a car and spent four weeks touring the three Hudson River counties in his electoral district, campaigning tirelessly. Despite the odds against him, Roosevelt won the election and took his seat in the state senate.

In 1912, Roosevelt ran for reelection and won again. During that election, Roosevelt also took the time to campaign for the Democratic presidential candidate, Woodrow Wilson. After the election, Wilson rewarded Roosevelt by appointing him assistant secretary of the navy. Roosevelt gladly accepted the position. He resigned his seat in the state senate and moved to Washington, D.C.

FDR campaigned for a seat in the New York state senate in 1910.

As assistant secretary of the navy, Roosevelt reviewing a group of U.S. troops in France during World War I

A campaign button from 1920

FOR VICE PRESIDENT
FRANKLIN D. ROOSEVELT

The appointment was an especially satisfying one for Roosevelt: Fifteen years earlier, cousin Teddy had held the very same office. The position allowed Roosevelt to gain valuable firsthand knowledge of the workings of Washington politics. He also made important political contacts during his time there.

By 1920, Roosevelt was the rising star of the Democratic Party. That year, he resigned as assistant secretary to run for vice president with presidential candidate James Cox, the governor of Ohio. Few expected the team to win—U.S. citizens seemed to want a change from the Democrats after World War I (1914–1918). As expected, the Cox-Roosevelt ticket was soundly defeated by Republicans Warren Harding and Calvin Coolidge. Roosevelt returned to his Hyde Park home to plot his next move up the political ladder.

In August 1921, Roosevelt vacationed at his summer home on Campobello Island off New Brunswick, Canada. One afternoon, after a dip in the chilly Atlantic waters, Roosevelt began to feel tired and unwell. He noticed that his legs ached. Roosevelt went to bed early, hoping that a good rest would help him recover. The next morning, however, his condition had worsened. By nightfall, he could not move his legs at all.

Two weeks later, doctors told the thirty-nine-year-old Roosevelt that he had contracted poliomyelitis, also called **polio**. Polio, a serious infection caused by a virus, was a common disease in the early twentieth century. The disease usually struck children and could cause permanent paralysis.

Doctors at first believed that Roosevelt might regain some use of his legs. Determined to walk again, Roosevelt spent the next seven years undergoing often

Senator Roosevelt

As a state senator, Roosevelt fought for bills that aided New York farmers and promoted conservation. In 1911, he made headlines across the nation when he dared to take on Tammany Hall. Tammany Hall was a powerful organization that controlled Democratic politics in New York State. The leader, or "boss," of this political machine called all the shots. The boss even used his influence to choose who would be the next U.S. senator from New York. Although it could have meant the end of his political career in the state, Roosevelt took a stand against the Tammany boss. He argued that New York's senator should be selected by the voters, not by Tammany Hall. Although he wasn't completely successful in his campaign against Tammany Hall, Roosevelt seemed to enjoy the battle. "There is nothing I love as much as a good fight," he said.

Roosevelt swimming in Warm Springs, Georgia

Later in his life, Roosevelt took time to visit young patients at the Warm Springs Foundation.

painful physical therapy and daily exercise. One of his favorite ways to exercise was swimming in the warm, soothing mineral waters at Warm Springs, Georgia. Roosevelt eventually established the Warm Springs Foundation, a center for the treatment of polio.

Despite his best efforts, Roosevelt never walked again. For the rest of his life, he spent much of his time in a wheelchair, yet many Americans never knew the extent of Roosevelt's disability. With a pair of heavy steel braces to support his legs, Roosevelt could stand upright, and with the help of a cane and the supporting arm of one of his sons, he could propel his hips forward, one at a time, giving the illusion of walking. Newspaper reporters rarely mentioned Roosevelt's paralysis, while cameramen and photographers never showed him in his wheelchair. This was the way Roosevelt wanted it. "No sob stuff," he told reporters.

After Roosevelt's illness, his mother, Sara, wanted him to return to Hyde Park and retire from politics, but Roosevelt refused to be locked away. With Eleanor acting as his eyes and ears, he kept in touch with what was happening in the world. Soon, Roosevelt began planning his return to politics.

At the 1924 Democratic National Convention, Roosevelt made his first public appearance since becoming ill. Leaning on a crutch with one arm and supported by son James on the other, Roosevelt carefully made his way to the podium. The crowd applauded wildly as he delivered the nominating speech for New York governor Alfred E. Smith. Most people would never know how much effort it took for Roosevelt to stand there and deliver the speech. Only those closest to him saw how

Learning Courage

After he was stricken with polio, Franklin Roosevelt worked hard to recover. Every day, he exercised to strengthen his arms and upper body. He practiced using wooden crutches and steel braces to support himself, and even though these contraptions often caused him great pain, he kept his positive outlook and sense of humor throughout the ordeal.

Many people who knew Roosevelt felt that his battle with polio had somehow added something important, even heroic, to his character. Others believed that it served to enhance qualities that were already there.

Eleanor Roosevelt believed that her husband's illness had strengthened him and taught him courage. She said, "I know that he had real fear when he was first taken ill, but he learned to surmount it. After that, I never heard him say he was afraid of anything."

Governor Roosevelt in 1929

tightly he gripped the podium for support. Roosevelt's appearance was the highlight of the convention.

Four years later, Smith once again sought—and this time won—the top slot on the Democratic presidential ticket. Smith pressed Roosevelt to run for his old job: governor of New York. Although Roosevelt was at first reluctant, he eventually accepted the challenge.

To prove his fitness, Roosevelt campaigned tirelessly for himself and for Smith throughout New York. To the voters who saw him speak, Roosevelt never appeared tired, weak, or unfit. When he was asked about his legs, Roosevelt would reply, "Do I look like a sick man?"

Roosevelt won the governor's seat by a very narrow margin. In his new role, he quickly began to make a name for himself. During his first two years in office, Roosevelt helped create laws to aid farmers and to reform New York's banks. Then, in October 1929, the New York Stock Exchange crashed. This event marked the beginning of the Great Depression and signaled dark days ahead for New York—and America.

The Great Depression, which lasted from 1929 through the early 1940s, was the most severe economic crisis the United States had ever faced. Millions of people lost their jobs as factories and other businesses closed down. Thousands of banks across the country were forced out of business as people rushed to withdraw their savings. Many families lost their farms and their homes.

Lines of unemployed people at a New York City soup kitchen during the Great Depression

Depression-Era Governor

As governor of New York, Roosevelt worked to help victims of the Great Depression. He set up such innovative state agencies as TERA to give direct relief to those in trouble. He also increased the state income tax, a move that made him unpopular with many New Yorkers. In 1931, Roosevelt explained his actions: "It is clear to me that it is the duty of those who have benefited by our industrial and economic system to come to the front in such a grave emergency and assist in relieving those who, under the same industrial and economic order, are the losers and sufferers."

After Roosevelt was reelected governor in 1930, he turned his attention to easing the Depression in his state. Roosevelt knew that he must help those people suffering the effects of the economic crisis. "The progress of our civilization will be retarded if any large body of citizens falls behind," he said. In 1931, he established the Temporary Emergency Relief Administration (TERA). TERA was the first state **agency** to assist unemployed Depression victims.

During his second term as governor, Roosevelt formed a group that came to be known as the Brain Trust. Noted professors, writers, and others advised Roosevelt and helped him develop new policies and solutions to the problems of the Great Depression. Later, when Roosevelt became president, he brought the Brain Trust with him to Washington, D.C.

Although Roosevelt enjoyed the challenges of being governor of New York, he still wanted more. In 1932, he set his sights on the most important political position in the nation: the presidency.

A NEW DEAL FOR AMERICA

In 1932, the Great Depression was taking a serious toll on people across the nation. More than 12 million Americans were out of work, and thousands of families had lost their homes. Some of the homeless moved to tent cities, shantytowns that were called "Hoovervilles," after Republican president Herbert Hoover.

President Hoover had hoped the nation would pull itself out of the depression. He believed that the government should take only limited action to help the economy recover. Other people disagreed. They criticized Hoover for not acting quickly to help those in need. Many Americans began to blame him for not being able to end the Great Depression.

The Democrats knew that the person they nominated to run for president would have a very good chance of beating Hoover in the fall. After bitter debate and much political wrangling, Roosevelt was chosen as the right man for the job. Texan John Nance Garner was chosen as his running mate.

Roosevelt immediately broke with tradition by flying out to the Democratic convention in Chicago to accept the nomination in person. In his acceptance speech, Roosevelt said, "I pledge you, I pledge myself, to a **New Deal** for the American people." He asked voters to "give me your help, not to win votes alone, but to win in this crusade to restore America to its own people."

Many people blamed President Hoover for the problems of the Great Depression.

President Hoover and the Great Depression

While some Americans found it easy to place the blame for the Great Depression on President Hoover, the causes of this serious crisis were much more complex. Over-production of manufactured goods, an unregulated banking system, and a volatile stock market all played a part in causing the depression. An underlying problem was that a very small number of people in the United States controlled most of the nation's riches. This created an ever-increasing gap between the rich and the poor.

Years after Hoover left office, he recalled the time when shantytowns bore his name and people booed him and pelted his car with rotten eggs. He said, "Once upon a time my political opponents honored me as possessing the fabulous intellectual and economic power by which I created a worldwide depression all by myself."

Many Democratic leaders encouraged Roosevelt to stay at home and let Garner do the campaigning. They were afraid that Roosevelt's disability would prove a liability in the election. Roosevelt, however, was determined to show the American people that he was a healthy, vital candidate for the presidency. Over the next few months, Roosevelt toured the country by train. He swept through thirty-eight states, winning support everywhere he went.

With his infectious grin and sunny optimism, Roosevelt gave the people of the United States something they were sorely in need of—hope. Even Roosevelt's campaign song, "Happy Days Are Here Again," underscored his message. Everywhere he went, he promised his New Deal for the American people.

Roosevelt traveled by train to campaign for the 1932 presidential election.

"A Pleasant Man"

Not everyone thought Roosevelt was the right person to pull the country out of the Great Depression. One journalist, Walter Lippmann, wrote the following assessment of Roosevelt before the 1932 Democratic convention:

[Roosevelt] is a highly impressionable person, without a firm grasp of public affairs, and without very strong convictions . . . an amiable man with many philanthropic impulses, but he is not the dangerous enemy of anything. He is too eager to please. . . . Franklin D. Roosevelt is no crusader. He is no tribune of the people. He is no enemy of entrenched privilege. He is a pleasant man who, without any important qualifications for the office, would very much like to be president.

An exuberant Roosevelt delivering a 1932 campaign speech in Kansas

Although some politicians and reporters criticized Roosevelt's general, often vague, statements, the public loved him.

On Election Day, Roosevelt beat Hoover by 7 million votes. He won 57.4 percent of the popular vote, capturing forty-two out of forty-eight states. Roosevelt was elated. He believed that the people had spoken, and what they wanted was change.

Assassination Attempt

On February 15, 1933, Roosevelt was visiting Miami, Florida. As the president-elect talked with Mayor Anton Cermak of Chicago, an Italian immigrant named Guiseppe Zangara (left, shown in jail) approached the two men. Zangara pulled out a gun and began firing at Roosevelt. All the shots missed Roosevelt, but Cermak was mortally wounded. Four others were also injured in the attack. Although Secret Service agents rushed Roosevelt away in his car, the president-elect made them return to help the injured. Zangara was executed on March 20, 1933.

On March 4, 1933, the United States was in the very depths of the Great Depression. Unemployment had increased in the four months since the election. Thousands of U.S. banks had closed, put out of business as panicked customers tried to withdraw all their funds. Yet, on that day, millions of Americans felt hopeful as Franklin Delano Roosevelt became the nation's thirty-second president.

Roosevelt's inauguration as thirty-second president of the United States on March 4, 1933

The inauguration ceremony took place on a bitter-cold winter day. Thousands of Americans had gathered in front of the Capitol to hear the new president speak. They watched in silence as Roosevelt slowly made his way to the podium on the arm of his son James. In a clear, ringing voice, Roosevelt took the oath of office. Then, as millions of Americans across the nation listened by radio, Roosevelt delivered his inaugural speech.

In the speech, Roosevelt sought to calm and reassure the American public. "The only thing we have to fear is fear itself," he told listeners. Roosevelt promised to put unemployed Americans back to work and provide relief for the needy. He also promised that the United States would be a good neighbor to other nations of

WPA programs employed workers in a variety of fields.

the world, by assisting them and working cooperatively with them.

One of Roosevelt's first acts as president was to call Congress into a special session. From March 9 to June 16, Congress passed a number of new laws aimed at helping the United States recover from the Depression. These **relief and reform programs** became known as Roosevelt's New Deal. Relief and reform programs aided citizens and improved the way businesses and industries were operated. Never before had the federal government assumed such responsibility for its citizens.

Alphabet Soup

Between 1933 and 1936, Roosevelt and Congress created relief and reform agencies that were nicknamed the "alphabet agencies." The agencies included:

AAA—Agricultural Adjustment Act: helped farmers by raising crop prices

CCC—Civilian Conservation Corps: provided jobs for unmarried young men

FDIC—Federal Deposit Insurance Corporation: protected depositors by insuring all bank deposits up to $100,000

FERA—Federal Emergency Relief Administration: gave millions of dollars to states for relief efforts; provided employment for thousands of people

NIRA—National Industrial Recovery Act: regulated industry and allowed workers to form unions

PWA—Public Works Administration: sponsored large-scale construction projects

TVA—Tennessee Valley Authority: built dams that supplied electricity to thousands of poor people in seven states

New Deal legislation created jobs for the unemployed and helped people complete their educations. It provided aid for farmers and laborers. And the New Deal helped regulate industry and banking. Roosevelt's first 100 days set a standard for productivity that other presidents have tried to emulate through the years. Today, reporters and writers often talk about what a new president has done during his first 100 days in office.

THE SECOND NEW DEAL

Beginning in the spring of 1935, Roosevelt and Congress passed a number of new programs that came to be known as the second New Deal. From 1935 through 1941, three major acts were passed and implemented:

A 1935 poster advertising a Works Progress art exhibit

• The Works Progress Administration (WPA) created jobs for more than 8.5 million unemployed Americans from 1935 to 1943. Laborers built roads, bridges, libraries, and schools. Artists, writers, and musicians were given jobs, too. The WPA was the largest job program for unemployed Americans.

• The Wagner Act, also called the National Labor Relations Act, guaranteed labor organizations the right to bargain with management. The act fostered the growth of labor organizations in the 1930s and 1940s.

• The Social Security Act was one of the most important

The Works Progress Administration

Artists, musicians, and writers were among the 8.5 million people who benefited from the Works Progress Administration (WPA). Beginning in 1935, artists were paid to paint murals on the walls of government buildings throughout the nation. Writers were hired to interview former slaves and create travel guides for each state. Actors and musicians performed for people living in urban and rural areas. Others recorded oral history, native folk tales, and songs.

Not all of the workers hired by the WPA were artists, of course. In the eight years it existed, the WPA built 650,000 miles (1,046 kilometers) of road, 125,000 buildings, and 75,000 bridges. WPA workers also served hot lunches to schoolchildren, taught adult literacy courses, and provided medical and dental services to the poor. The WPA was abolished by Congress in 1943.

Roosevelt's Fireside Chats helped calm the U.S. people as well as inform them about important issues.

and long-lasting pieces of New Deal legislation. The act created old-age pensions and unemployment compensation as well as aid to the disabled and dependent children.

By the end of Roosevelt's first term, the U.S. economy was beginning to recover. Yet certain groups, especially business owners and the rich, were beginning to sharply criticize Roosevelt. They believed he was hurting industry in the United States by helping labor unions and overtaxing businesses and the wealthy. Many critics accused Roosevelt of creating a nation of people dependent upon **welfare**, or government aid. Some even went so far as to label him a **Socialist** or a **Communist**. Roosevelt's popularity with the people, however, was as strong as ever. There was no question that he would run for—and probably win—a second term in office.

Fireside Chats

On March 12, 1933, Roosevelt began a tradition that would continue throughout his twelve years in office: Fireside Chats. In his first chat, Roosevelt explained the recent banking crisis. In plain, simple language, the president both informed and calmed listeners.

I want to talk for a few minutes with the people of the United States about banking . . . I want to tell you what has been done in the last few days, why it was done, and what the next steps are going to be. . . .

We had a bad banking situation. Some of our bankers had shown themselves either incompetent or dishonest in their handling of the people's funds. They had used the money entrusted to them in speculations and unwise loans. This was of course not true in the vast majority of our banks but it was true in enough of them to shock the people for a time into a sense of insecurity. . . . It was the government's job to straighten out this situation and do it as quickly as possible—and the job is being performed.

Roosevelt finished his chat on a reassuring note, "Together we cannot fail."

CHAPTER 5

TROUBLE ON THE HORIZON

In the 1936 election, Roosevelt's Republican opponent was Governor Alfred Landon of Kansas. Roosevelt won by another landslide, this time attaining 60.8 percent of the popular vote. In his second inaugural speech, made on January 20, 1937, he reminded Americans of the progress that had been made over the last four years. Roosevelt also acknowledged that there was still a long way to go. "I see one-third of a nation ill-housed, ill-clad, ill-nourished," he said.

A victorious FDR, along with Franklin Jr. and Eleanor, on election night 1936

The president was at the height of his popularity. The only thing that seemed to be standing in his way was the Supreme Court. All the justices were men who had been appointed by past presidents. Four were very conservative and strongly opposed Roosevelt's New Deal. The court had already overturned some of the most important New Deal legislation, saying that it violated the Constitution. The justices felt that programs such as the AAA and the NIRA infringed upon states' rights and went too far in providing aid to needy Americans.

Roosevelt wanted to appoint justices who would support his New Deal. He came up with a plan that would allow justices who were seventy or older to retire at full pay. If they refused, Roosevelt would appoint additional, new justices to sit on the Court with them.

Running for Reelection

In his first term as president, Roosevelt went after big business and the wealthy. He established controls in many industries and raised the taxes of the wealthiest people in the nation. When Roosevelt accepted the nomination for a second term, he spoke about these issues. "The economic royalists complain that we seek to overthrow the institutions of America. What they really complain of is that we seek to take away their power. Our allegiance to American institutions requires the overthrow of this kind of power." Roosevelt continued, "There is a mysterious cycle in human events. To some generations, much is given. Of other generations, much is expected. This generation of Americans has a rendezvous with destiny."

Later in the campaign, Roosevelt spelled out one of his goals for his second term. "I should like to have it said of my first administration that in it the forces of selfishness and of lust for power met their match," he said. "I should like to have it said of my second administration that in it these forces met their master."

The plan could have increased the number of Supreme Court justices by six.

Roosevelt didn't anticipate the public outcry that erupted when he revealed his new plan. Reporters, congressmen, and even the U.S. public began calling the president's idea a "court-packing plan." They said Roosevelt was trying to get around the checks and balances provided in the Constitution.

As Roosevelt tried to gather support for his plan, he was dealt two blows. First, the Supreme Court came out in favor of some of Roosevelt's New Deal legislation. Second, one of the older, more conservative justices announced his retirement. Considered unnecessary—perhaps unconstitutional—Roosevelt's plan was soundly defeated in Congress. Roosevelt lost some of his popularity with the public by pushing the issue.

A WORLD AT WAR

During his second term in office, Roosevelt turned his attention to problems outside the United States. Three nations—Italy, Japan, and Germany—were invading weaker nations. In 1935, Italy invaded Ethiopia; in 1937, Japan captured much of China. Then, in September 1939, **Nazi** Germany, under the leadership of Adolf Hitler, attacked Poland. Then Great

German dictator
Adolf Hitler in 1939

Britain and France immediately declared war on Germany, marking the beginning of World War II.

Roosevelt knew that, at this time, most Americans wanted to stay out of the conflict. **Isolationists**, people who did not want to become involved, were against providing aid to any of the countries at war, including Great Britain and France. They believed that aiding these countries would draw the United States into the war. Many isolationists, including the famous pilot Charles Lindbergh, believed that the nation should only fight battles that directly affected its economic interests or threatened its borders.

Keeping America Out of War

In 1936, Roosevelt hoped to keep the United States out of war. Roosevelt had seen the horrors of World War I battlefields when he visited Europe in 1918. He later said, "I have seen war. I have seen war on land and on sea. I have seen blood running from the wounded. I have seen men coughing out their gassed lungs. I have seen the dead in the mud. I have seen cities destroyed. . . . I have seen children starving. I have seen the agony of mothers and wives. I hate war."

Roosevelt felt strongly that the United States should provide aid to Great Britain, France, and China, the nations fighting against Germany, Italy, and Japan (the **Axis powers**). In 1939, after Germany invaded Poland, Roosevelt succeeded in persuading Congress to revise the Neutrality Acts. These acts called for the United States to stay out of all foreign entanglements and to provide no aid to nations at war. Roosevelt's revisions allowed the United States to begin selling arms to Great Britain and other **Allied powers**.

Roosevelt, supported by his son James, after addressing Congress in 1939

A THIRD TERM?

As the next election drew closer, people across the nation wondered if Roosevelt would run for a third term. There was, as yet, no law forbidding a president from doing so. However, presidents traditionally served only two terms in office.

For months, Roosevelt kept the nation—and even his own advisers—in suspense by wavering in his decision. Some say he did so just to keep other Democrats from pursuing the nomination. At one point, it was rumored that he even agreed to take a job as an editor at *Collier's* magazine for the year following the election. In spite of all this indecision, at the Democratic convention in July 1940, Roosevelt accepted the nomination for his third term as president. With the threat of war hanging over the nation, he wanted to be the person leading the United States. Roosevelt would run for an unprecedented—and controversial—third term.

CHAPTER 6

During the 1940 campaign, the Republicans nominated businessman Wendell Willkie to run against Roosevelt. Willkie believed that no man should be elected to three terms as president. He and his supporters felt that this might lead to a dictatorship in the United States. American voters disagreed. In November, Roosevelt beat Willkie with 55 percent of the popular vote.

Roosevelt's third inaugural speech focused on the increasingly dangerous world crisis. He warned Americans that, in the face of Nazi aggression, much was at stake. "In the face of great perils never before encountered," he said, "our strong purpose is to protect and to perpetuate the integrity of democracy."

The tide of public opinion about the war had begun to change even before the 1940 election. That spring, Germany invaded Denmark, Norway, the Netherlands, Belgium, and France. Germany's aggressive actions shocked the American people. The United States began to prepare for war. In the summer, Congress approved money to strengthen the armed forces. It also passed the first peacetime draft bill. The bill required all men between the ages of twenty-one and thirty-six to register for military training.

German troops marching through Denmark in 1940

Helping Your Neighbors

At a White House press conference, Roosevelt explained the Lend-Lease Act: "Suppose my neighbor's home catches fire . . . I don't say to him . . . 'Neighbor, my garden hose cost me $15; you have to pay me $15 for it.' . . . I don't want $15—I want my garden hose back after the fire is over." In simple words, Roosevelt was telling Americans that the Allies desperately needed help in their fight against the Axis powers—and that the United States must respond quickly.

The Atlantic Charter

In August 1941, Roosevelt met secretly with British prime minister Winston Churchill on a ship off the coast of Canada. During the meeting, Roosevelt agreed that U.S. warships would escort British ships through North Atlantic waters. This would offer the British vessels some protection against German submarines, called U-boats. Together, the two men also worked out what came to be known as the Atlantic Charter. The charter detailed the two nations' war aims and laid out what came to be called the four freedoms: freedom of worship and speech and freedom from fear or want.

After Roosevelt's inauguration, Congress passed the Lend-Lease Act. This act allowed the United States to provide military aid to countries that were victims of aggression—even if those nations didn't have the money to pay for the aid. The act benefited Great Britain and, later, the Soviet Union. "We must be the great **arsenal** for democracy," Roosevelt declared.

One by-product of the Lend-Lease Act was an increase in manufacturing throughout the United States. As new factories were built to meet the increased demand, millions of new jobs were created. This marked the beginning of the end of the Great Depression.

A DAY OF INFAMY

On December 7, 1941, the United States found itself thrust into the war. The Japanese, hoping to enlarge their empire in the Pacific and angered by U.S. trade **embargoes**, attacked Pearl Harbor, a U.S. naval base in Hawaii. Without warning, Japanese warplanes bombed

U.S. ships and aircraft, crippling the U.S. Pacific Fleet. More than 2,300 Americans were killed in the attack.

After the bombing, some Americans blamed Roosevelt for not anticipating the attack on Pearl Harbor. Relations between Japan and the United States had been deteriorating since 1940. In fact, U.S. Army forces had decoded secret messages from Japan to their ambassador in the United States. These messages

The attack on Pearl Harbor on December 7, 1941, marked the U.S. entrance into World War II.

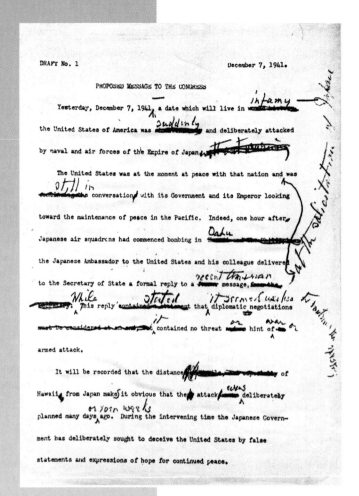

DRAFT No. 1   December 7, 1941.

PROPOSED MESSAGE TO THE CONGRESS

Yesterday, December 7, 1941, a date which will live in ~~world history~~ *infamy*

the United States of America was *suddenly* and deliberately attacked

by naval and air forces of the Empire of Japan.

The United States was at the moment at peace with that nation and was
still in conversation with its Government and its Emperor looking

toward the maintenance of peace in the Pacific. Indeed, one hour after,

Japanese air squadrons had commenced bombing in *Oahu*

the Japanese Ambassador to the United States and his colleague delivered

to the Secretary of State a formal reply to a *recent American* message.

While This reply *stated* *it seemed useless* that diplomatic negotiations

it *on war or* contained no threat or hint of

armed attack.

It will be recorded that the distance of

Hawaii from Japan makes it obvious that the attack *was* deliberately

planned many days ago. During the intervening time the Japanese Govern-

ment has deliberately sought to deceive the United States by false

statements and expressions of hope for continued peace.

A draft of Roosevelt's famous speech to Congress on December 8, 1941, that requested a declaration of war against Japan

implied that an attack on the United States was imminent. Based on the reports, most top officials, Roosevelt included, believed that the Japanese would certainly attack. But no one believed they would attack Pearl Harbor. They felt it was too far from Japan.

The day after the attack, Roosevelt addressed a joint session of Congress, asking for a declaration of war against Japan. He called December 7 "a date which will live in infamy." Congress quickly granted Roosevelt's request, with only one member voting against the declaration of war. In the days that followed, Germany and Italy both declared war on the United States. The United States had entered World War II.

COMMANDER IN CHIEF

For the first few months after the United States entered the war, there were few victories. In the summer of 1942, the tide began to turn. On August 28, U.S. forces defeated the Japanese at the Battle of Midway, an important naval battle in the Pacific Ocean. In November, U.S. troops joined British troops in driving Germany out of North Africa. That winter, the Russians also began to force the Germans from their lands.

In 1943, Allied troops began to focus on Western Europe. In July, the Allies invaded Italy, taking control of most of the country. The battle to liberate the rest of Western Europe began on "D-Day"—June 6, 1944. That day, thousands of Allied troops landed on French soil in Normandy.

During the war, Roosevelt was a strong commander in chief. With leaders of other Allied nations, the president helped decide battle strategy and formulate peace policies. In 1943, Roosevelt became the first president to leave the country during wartime. That year, he met with Britain's prime minister Winston Churchill in French Morocco, Africa. At the Casablanca Conference,

The front page of the *Los Angeles Times* on December 8, 1941

America at War

During a Fireside Chat on December 9, 1941, Roosevelt told Americans that they were at war against Japan. "We are now in this war," Roosevelt said. "We are all in it—all the way. Every single man, woman, and child is a partner in the most tremendous undertaking of our American history. We must share together the bad news and the good news, the defeats and the victories, the changing fortunes of war."

The president went on to talk about the tough times that lay ahead for the United States. "On the road ahead there lies hard work, grueling work, day and night, every hour and every minute," he said. "I was about to add that ahead there lies sacrifice for all of us. But it is not correct to use that word. The United States does not consider it a sacrifice to do all one can, to give one's best to our nation when the nation is fighting for its existence and its future."

Roosevelt finished on an optimistic note. "So we are going to win the war," he said, "and we are going to win the peace that follows. And in the difficult hours of this day, through dark days that may be yet to come, we will know that the vast majority of the members of the human race are on our side."

Allied troops landed at Normandy on June 6, 1944.

the two leaders pledged to form an international peacekeeping organization once the war had ended. This organization would one day come to be known as the United Nations.

In 1943, Roosevelt, Churchill, and Soviet leader Joseph Stalin met together for the first time. At the Tehran Conference in Iran, the "Big Three" agreed to the upcoming invasion of France. Stalin also agreed to help the Allies defeat Japan once the war against Germany was won.

Roosevelt and the Holocaust

One of the harshest criticisms about President Roosevelt's wartime leadership concerned his reaction to the **Holocaust**. The Holocaust was the systematic killing of Jewish people throughout Europe by the Nazis. From 1939 to 1945, 6 million Jews and millions of other Europeans, including Gypsies, Slavs, people with disabilities, and political and religious leaders, were killed by the Germans. Most died in **concentration camps**, prisons run by the Nazis. Many of Roosevelt's contemporaries felt that the president should have done much more to stop this **genocide** (the annihilation of a specific race or culture). Critics felt that Roosevelt too rigidly enforced immigration quotas that allowed only a certain number of people from each country to enter the United States. Once the United States was involved in the war, Roosevelt refused to give orders to bomb gas chambers and railway lines used to take prisoners to death camps. He felt that such actions would endanger the lives of too many innocent civilians. Although Roosevelt did initiate a rescue program in 1944, many believed that it was too little, too late. The program, called the War Refugee Board, helped save 200,000 Jewish refugees.

WORKING FOR PEACE

In 1944, Roosevelt decided that he must run for a fourth term in office. Although he was tired and ailing, he felt that he should see the war through to the end. Democratic leaders agreed, but they encouraged Roosevelt to choose Harry S. Truman as his running mate. They wanted to make sure that a strong, moderate leader would replace Roosevelt if he became ill in office.

In November, Roosevelt won his fourth presidential election. He defeated New York governor Thomas Dewey by the closest margin yet, with 53.5 percent of the vote. Roosevelt's inauguration address, delivered in January 1945, was one of the shortest any president had ever given. In it, Roosevelt said that Americans had learned

Harry Truman (left) was chosen as Roosevelt's running mate for the 1944 election.

Fala Takes Offense

During Roosevelt's presidential campaign, he took the time to poke fun at his opponents. In September 1944, the president used humor and his little Scottish terrier, Fala (right), to make a point. "These Republican leaders have not been content with attacks on me, or my wife, or on my sons," Roosevelt said. "No, not content with that, they now include my little dog, Fala. Well, of course, I don't resent the attacks and my family doesn't resent the attacks, but Fala does resent them."

Roosevelt's inauguration in 1945

The Road to Peace

After the Yalta Conference, Roosevelt made his last address to Congress. In his speech, the president talked about the prospects for future peace.

The structure of world peace cannot be the work of one man, or one party, or one nation . . . it must be a peace which rests on the cooperative effort of the whole world. Peace can endure only so long as humanity really insists on it, and is willing to work for and sacrifice for it.

The "Big Three"—Churchill, FDR, and Stalin—meeting in Yalta in February 1945

that "we cannot live alone, at peace; that our own well-being is dependent on the well-being of other nations far away."

Both the war and the campaign took a heavy toll on Roosevelt's health. In 1944, a physical examination showed that Roosevelt was suffering from dangerous heart and circulatory problems. Doctors warned Roosevelt to quit smoking, watch his diet, and avoid stress whenever possible. The American people, however, were told that Roosevelt was healthy.

Despite his health problems, Roosevelt journeyed to Yalta in the Soviet Union shortly after his inauguration in 1945. At the Yalta Conference, the Big Three met once again. They began to work out the fine details of the United Nations. Roosevelt believed that the United Nations would guarantee future world peace. "The United Nations will evolve into the best method ever devised for stopping war," he said.

When Roosevelt returned to the United States from Yalta, friends and advisers who saw him were shocked at how ill he looked. He seemed weak and frail, and during an appearance in Congress, Roosevelt even sat while making a speech. "I hope you will pardon me for an unusual posture of sitting down," he said, "But I know that you will realize that it makes it a lot easier for me in not having to carry about ten pounds of steel around on the bottom of my legs and also because I have just completed a 14,000-mile [22,526-km] trip."

At the end of March, Roosevelt left for a vacation at Warm Springs, Georgia. He hoped that the time away from Washington would help him relax and regain his health. In Georgia, Roosevelt was met by two of his cousins and Lucy Mercer, now Lucy Rutherford. Over the years, Roosevelt had maintained a relationship with Rutherford, despite his promise to Eleanor never to see his mistress again.

After a few days away from Washington, D.C., Roosevelt began to look and feel better. On April 12, the president was having his portrait painted. At 12:45, he

Roosevelt's casket near the burial site at Hyde Park, New York

An End to War

Franklin Roosevelt didn't live long enough to see the end of World War II. Less than one month after the president's death, Allied forces marched into Berlin. Hitler had already committed suicide, and Germany swiftly surrendered. Great Britain and the United States declared May 8, 1945, to be V-E Day—Victory in Europe Day. The war in the Pacific, however, continued into the summer. In August 1945, U.S. planes dropped atomic bombs on the Japanese cities of Hiroshima and Nagasaki. Estimates of Japanese killed ranged from 80,000 to 200,000 in Hiroshima alone. On September 2, 1945, Japan officially surrendered, bringing World War II to a close.

looked at his watch and told the painter, "We have fifteen more minutes to work." Fifteen minutes later, Roosevelt put his hand to his head and said, "I have a terrific headache." Then he slumped over. The president had suffered a massive cerebral hemorrhage. He died less than three hours later.

Thousands of people lined the tracks as a train brought Roosevelt's body back to Washington, D.C. In the capital, thousands more watched as Roosevelt's coffin was carried down Pennsylvania Avenue. Roosevelt was finally laid to rest in the rose garden of his home in Hyde Park, New York.

ROOSEVELT'S LEGACY

Although Roosevelt had been ill in his last months, people all over the world were surprised and saddened by his death. When asked about Roosevelt, Winston Churchill told a reporter, "One day the world, and history, will know what it owes to your president."

Roosevelt's legacy lives on. Such New Deal measures as Social Security, unemployment compensation, and public housing continue to assist people today. The federal government continues to regulate the banking industry and the stock market using measures started during Roosevelt's presidency.

Roosevelt also led the nation through two of the worst periods in U.S. history. When he died, the Great Depression was over, and the end of World War II was in sight. The United Nations, the peacekeeping organization that Roosevelt had dreamed of, would meet for the first time shortly after his death, and Eleanor Roosevelt was one of the first U.S. delegates to the United Nations.

Throughout his twelve years as president, Roosevelt's courage and optimism sustained the American people through times of crisis. His faith in America and the American people may be Roosevelt's greatest legacy.

During his presidency, Franklin D. Roosevelt created programs and agencies that made the United States a stronger country.

Franklin Delano Roosevelt Memorial

On May 2, 1997, President Bill Clinton dedicated the Franklin Delano Roosevelt Memorial in Washington, D.C. The memorial covers more than 7 acres (2.8 hectares). It is made up of four separate areas that symbolize Roosevelt's four terms as president. The rooms are filled with images of the president, as well as excerpts from many of his important speeches.

TIMELINE

1882	Franklin Delano Roosevelt is born on January 30 in Hyde Park, New York
1896	Enters Groton School in Groton, Massachusetts
1900	Enters Harvard University
1904	Enters Columbia Law School
1905	Marries distant cousin Anna Eleanor Roosevelt on March 17
1910	Elected to the New York state senate
1913	Appointed assistant secretary of the navy
1920	Runs unsuccessfully for vice president
1921	Becomes ill with polio and permanently loses the use of his legs
1927	Founds the Warm Springs Foundation
1928	Nominates Alfred E. Smith for president at the Democratic National Convention; elected governor of New York
1932	Elected thirty-second president of the United States
1933	Takes the oath of office on March 4
1936	Elected to a second term as president
1940	Elected to a third term as president
1941	Meets secretly with Winston Churchill to draw up the Atlantic Charter; declares war on Japan after the bombing of Pearl Harbor
1943	Meets Churchill in Africa at the Casablanca Conference; meets Churchill and Stalin in Iran at the Tehran Conference
1944	Elected to a fourth term as president
1945	Attends the Yalta Conference; dies at Warm Springs, Georgia, on April 12

agency: a government department that performs a specific task or tasks

Allied powers: the nations that fought against Germany, Italy, and Japan during World War II, including Great Britain, the Soviet Union, France, and the United States

arsenal: a place where weapons are made and stored

Axis powers: the three nations the United States opposed during World War II: Germany, Italy, and Japan

Communist: a person who believes that all property should be owned by the government and shared equally by all citizens

concentration camp: a prison camp where political prisoners and refugees are held

embargoes: government orders that ban trade with another country

genocide: the deliberate destruction of a race or culture of people

Great Depression: a period of severe economic distress in the United States that lasted from 1929 to 1941

Holocaust: the mass extermination of six million European Jews by the Nazis during World War II

isolationists: people who believe that the United States should not get involved in foreign situations

Nazi: a member of Adolf Hitler's Nazi Party of the 1930s and 1940s; Germany, under Nazi control, initiated World War II.

New Deal: national relief and recovery legislation passed by Congress and signed by Roosevelt during his first term in office

polio: an infection, caused by a virus, that can cause paralysis. A vaccine for polio was developed in the 1950s.

relief and reform programs: New Deal programs that helped citizens and improved the way businesses and industries operated

Socialist: a person who believes that a nation's industries should be controlled by the state or groups of workers

Soviet Union: the union of Communist countries in Eastern Europe and Northwest Asia, including Russia. Formed in 1922 after World War I, the Soviet Union broke apart in 1991.

welfare: government aid provided to people in need

TO FIND OUT MORE

BOOKS

Ambrose, Stephen E. *The Good Fight: How World War II Was Won.* New York: Atheneum Books for Young Readers, 2001.

Collier, Christopher, and James Lincoln Collier. *Progressivism, the Great Depression, and the New Deal.* Tarrytown, N.Y.: Benchmark Books, 2001.

Freedman, Russell. *Franklin Delano Roosevelt.* New York: Clarion Books, 1990.

Morey, Eileen. *Eleanor Roosevelt.* San Diego: Lucent Books, 1998.

Nishi, Dennis. *Life During the Great Depression.* San Diego: Lucent Books, 1998.

INTERNET SITES

The American President
www.americanpresident.org
Filled with information on Roosevelt and other U.S. presidents.

Avalon Project
http://www.yale.edu/lawweb/avalon/20th.htm
For primary-source material relating to Roosevelt's presidency, including transcripts of his inauguration speeches.

Fireside Chat Transcripts
http://www.mhric.org/fdr/fdr.html
For full transcripts of Roosevelt's many Fireside Chats.

Franklin Delano Roosevelt Memorial
http://www.nps.gov/fdrm
For information about the FDR Memorial in Washington, D.C., as well as biographical information.

Franklin D. Roosevelt Library & Museum
http://www.fdrlibrary.marist.edu
Biographical information and other interesting Roosevelt resources.

New Deal Network
http://newdeal.feri.org
Includes photo, documents, and information about the Great Depression and the New Deal.

About the Author

Robin Doak has been writing for children for more than fourteen years. A former editor of *Weekly Reader* and *U*S*Kids* magazine, Doak has authored fun and educational materials for kids of all ages, including books about American immigration, natural disasters, hockey, chemistry, and nutrition. Doak lives with her husband and three children in central Connecticut.